-AUG-1995

msc

12556

ROTHERHAM PUBLIC LIBRARIES

DECADES

The SIXTIES

Edward Grey

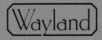
Wayland

DECADES

The Fifties
The Sixties
The Seventies
The Eighties

First published in 1989 by
Wayland (Publishers) Ltd
61 Western Road, Hove
East Sussex BN3 1JD, England

© Copyright 1989 Wayland (Publishers) Ltd

Edited by Roger Coote
Designed by Helen White
Series Consultant: Stuart Laing
Dean of Cultural and Community Studies
University of Sussex

British Library Cataloguing in Publication Data

The Sixties
1. Great Britain. Young persons.
Social Life 1945-
I. Title II. Series
941.085'088055

ISBN 1 85210 723 5

Typeset by Direct Image Photosetting Ltd
Hove, East Sussex, England
Printed in Italy by G. Canale and C.S.p.A., Turin
Bound in Belgium by Casterman S.A.

Contents

Introduction

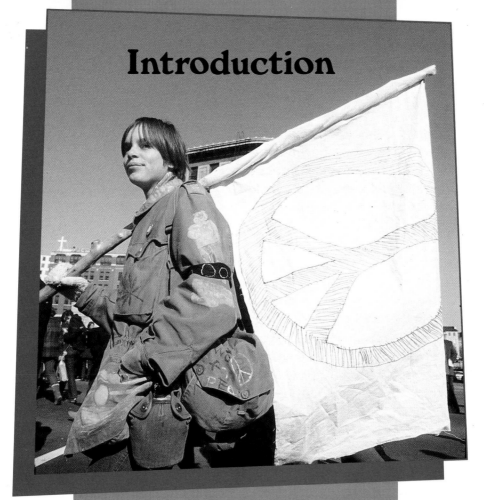

The period between 1960 and 1969 was the time of a teenage explosion. Young people were constantly in the news, whether through miniskirt fashions, pop groups such as the Beatles, hippy communes or student demonstrations. Even the adult world started to change in response. People spoke of a youth revolution. And it affected everything from music and clothes to sex, politics and religion.

The events bewildered many people at the time. What was going on? Looking back it is clear that several different factors lay behind the changes. For one thing, there was simply a very large number of teenagers in the world. After the Second World War (1939-45), millions of ex-servicemen and their wives had decided to start up families, creating a 'baby boom'. By the early sixties those boom babies had reached their teens.

Above A long-haired youth demonstrates against the Vietnam War during a huge protest march on Washington DC, November 1969.

As their parents prospered, the sixties teenagers found themselves with more money to spend. Youth clothing and music industries sprang up quickly to feed their interests. With plenty of jobs around, teenagers generally felt less need to fight for their survival in society than earlier generations had done. They had more time and leisure to question their parents' values and to explore different ways of life.

There were other explanations too. Teenagers in the sixties grew up with the real threat of a nuclear war as the background to their lives. It seemed possible that the world might come to an end before they came to be adults. This had two results. One was the desire to enjoy life immediately rather than wait for an uncertain future. The other was to turn decisively against warfare as a solution to problems.

Above An atomic test, photographed from above, at Bikini Atoll in the Pacific Ocean. Threat of nuclear war created anxiety, especially in the early sixties.

Below A teenage girl in the sixties. For many young women, miniskirts and long, loose hair symbolized new freedoms. Girls were permitted to treat their bodies with greater frankness than in earlier decades.

In the early sixties the Campaign for Nuclear Disarmament (CND) won wide support among young people in Britain. Later, when the United States became heavily involved in the Vietnam War (1959-73), thousands of young Americans refused to go and fight. There were demonstrations against the war throughout the western world. Student riots were widespread. Around 1968 it seemed as if the younger generation was in open revolt against the older.

So much has been written about the events that it is easy to forget the whole picture. Millions of teenagers still respected their parents, went to school, worried about exams, and met their first girlfriend or boyfriend. Most of them probably hoped to find a place in society sooner or later, and very few 'dropped out' completely. Nevertheless, attitudes and lifestyles did undergo a real transformation. The sixties were years of challenge and constant change.

Fashion

Around 1960 teenagers who wanted to look smart generally bought adult clothes. Young men were still expected to wear a 'sensible' jacket, with pressed trousers and a shirt and tie. Young women dressed much like their mothers, in whatever the big fashion houses and department stores decided was in style. Choice of casual wear was very limited. In the United States a range of jeans, T-shirts, zip-up jerkins and so on was available, but real American examples were hard to come by elsewhere.

Above The ultra thin 'Twiggy', a teenage fashion model, was one of Swinging London's most famous personalities.

Boutiques and miniskirts

It was around 1963 that things started to happen on the fashion front, and London was the centre of change. Increasing numbers of working teenagers had found themselves with money in their pockets and they were keen to spend it on records and clothes. Whilst the big stores kept turning out adult clothing, a number of smaller shops sprang up in London. They specialized in ready-to-wear clothing for the new youth market, and were called 'boutiques' (the French word for shops). Biba and Bus Stop were two examples. Another was Bazaar in the King's Road, Chelsea. It was run by Mary Quant, the most influential young fashion designer of the time.

The clothes were both imaginative and reasonably cheap. Fashion trends changed very fast, and 'trendy' became an 'in' word. For girls the great development was the miniskirt. In 1960 hemlines had been well below the knee but by 1965 they had risen to 15 cm above it. The fashion shocked many older people. It also brought about another significant change in women's fashion: miniskirts left so much leg showing that stockings became impractical, and Mary Quant introduced tights as a solution. For footwear to go with the mini, the French designer André Courreges introduced short white boots. Knee-length 'kinky boots' in suede or black leather came into style later.

Miniskirts were usually worn with a skimpy top, and sometimes with a see-through blouse. A bright plastic or PVC mac might be worn on top. In the mid-sixties the look was accompanied by heavy eye make-up, and sometimes false eyelashes. Hair might be back-combed or worn very long and straight. Some teenage girls even ironed their hair to obtain the perfect effect. The ideal was to look ultra young and slim. Girls who fitted it were known as 'dolly birds'.

The mini certainly allowed girls to treat their bodies with a new freedom and frankness. But feminists later objected to the 'dolly' idea: why should girls think of themselves as dolls for men to play with?

Left Skirts got shorter and shorter, and were sometimes made of throwaway plastic fabrics.

Fashion

Carnaby man

Changes in teenage menswear were even more startling, because colourful men's clothes had been unobtainable before. The heart of the revolution was London's Carnaby Street. While teenage boys started to grow their hair, combing it forward like the Beatles, a wealth of dandyish clothes started to appear. By the mid-sixties there were Regency-style jackets, striped hipster trousers and tab-collar shirts. Chelsea boots were worn, having elastic sides unlike ordinary lace-ups. 'Dutch-boy' caps were popular. In place of an ordinary shirt and tie, men often wore turtleneck sweaters, which came in a wide range of colours.

The main trend, though, was towards casualness. In the late sixties youth fashions had become so free that just about anything was acceptable. There were vogues for crushed velvet trousers, fringe waistcoats, cossack capes, military tunics, Indian kaftans and Mao jackets. Influenced by the hippies, some teenagers went around barefoot, and many boys grew their hair to shoulder length as a symbol of protest against adult society and authority.

Flared trousers suddenly became popular at the end of the decade and the style caught on so fast that the shops could not keep up with it. Teenagers sometimes split their straight jeans up to the knee, and filled in the gap with a triangular patch of material. Bell bottoms or loon pants, as they were also known, were often worn with a T-shirt that had been tie-dyed at home for psychedelic effect.

Below Military tunics displayed in a boutique called Gear on the Warpath. Anything with a Victorian or antique feel might be worn for fun, from long 'granny dresses' to old-fashioned muttonchop sideburns.

Above 'Dutch boy' caps worn by a young couple in the
United States. The caps were made popular by folk singers
such as Bob Dylan and Donovan. Notice also the
psychedelic patterning of the woman's dress. The man has
a decorative shirt and striped 'hipster' trousers.

Fashion

Above Rummaging for jeans at a boutique in London's King's Road, Chelsea. The interior is typically casual, with garments arranged on open racks or heaped in piles. Older clothing stores were much more formal.

The unisex look

One of the most important contributions to teenage style came from the United States — denim jeans. By 1969 they had become the perfect symbol of youth culture and were worn throughout the world. Levi's were the prized jeans. For the best effect, teenagers bought Levi's that were too large and then wore them in the bath so that the material shrank to fit.

Jeans were classless; that is, they gave no clue to a person's background, whether rich or poor. And they were sexless, too. A long-haired boy in jeans and a T-shirt looked much like a long-haired girl in jeans and a T-shirt. Adults complained that they couldn't tell them apart. But did that matter? By the time trouser-suits for girls appeared in the shops, people were already speaking of a

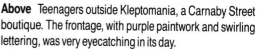

Above Teenagers outside Kleptomania, a Carnaby Street boutique. The frontage, with purple paintwork and swirling lettering, was very eyecatching in its day.

new unisex, or single sex, look.

Obviously not everyone wore the more extreme styles. But by the end of the decade lasting changes had occurred in the way people dressed. Boutiques had sprung up in most big cities, and even the department stores were selling ready-to-wear clothing especially for the teenage market. Adult men might be seen wearing a turtleneck with colourful cord trousers; adult women wore their skirts above the knee. The youth idea was triumphant. At the beginning of the sixties teenagers had wanted to look like adults; by the end adults wanted to look like teenagers.

# Pop Music

During the early sixties pop music was going through a quiet phase. The charts were mostly dominated by stars who had made their names in the fifties, and much of the rebelliousness had gone out of rock'n'roll.

There was, however, one craze that hinted at things to come. In 1961 a black singer called Chubby Checker had an international hit with *Let's Twist Again,* a song which launched a world-wide dance fad. The Twist involved a lot of energetic hip-wriggling that

Above Chubby Checker shows how to do the Twist. The great centre for twisters was the Peppermint Lounge, a club in New York City.

outraged some adults. And it started a new form of teenage dance in which couples faced one another but did not touch. Other dance crazes followed — the Watusi, the Swim, the Jerk, the Frug — all with the same feature in common. Teenagers no longer had to have a partner if they wanted to dance.

Beatlemania

The performers who seemed to change everything were the Beatles from Liverpool in England. Their first hit, *Love Me Do,* only crept up the British charts to number 17 in 1962. But they had an exciting new sound, based on a line-up of drums and three guitars. The pulsing of the bass guitar gave it an especially powerful 'beat' which began to catch on. The Beatles themselves were confident working-class youths with real song-writing talent and a lot of cheeky humour. Their distinctive 'mop-top' haircuts helped them stand out from other groups, and in 1963 they had a string of gigantic hits. The press wrote of 'Beatlemania'.

Above Twisting in the street. Many people believe that the craze caught on because it helped to release Cold War tensions in the early sixties. In this way it foreshadowed the 'freak outs' of later years.

Above The Beatles, from left to right Paul McCartney, George Harrison, Ringo Starr and John Lennon. In the early days the 'Fab Four' performed in sharply styled mod suits with distinctive round-neck collars.

When the group visited the United States in 1964 they had the same wild success. This was amazing, because until then America had always set the style in pop music. Other English guitar groups followed in the Beatles' wake: the Rolling Stones, the Animals, the Kinks and the Who were just a few. Like the Beatles they had all been strongly influenced by black American performers such as Little Richard, Bo Diddley and Chuck Berry. But because they were white youths they were able to reach a wider audience. They struck sexy, defiant attitudes which overwhelmed young fans everywhere. America and the rest of the western world were conquered by the 'English invasion'.

American sounds

Not all the big hits of the mid-sixties were English, however. In California the Beach Boys had created an exciting sound of their own, built around surf culture and hot rod cars. And black performers were starting to enter the charts on a regular basis through the Tamla Motown label. Founded in Detroit the Motown company rose to become the biggest black-owned business in America with a wealth of hits by the Supremes, the Four Tops, Smokey Robinson, Marvin Gaye, Stevie Wonder and many others.

The most influential songwriter of the time was also an American, Bob Dylan. He had

Above The Temptations, one of many highly successful Motown groups. The company was founded by songwriter Berry Gordy Junior in 1962, and four years later was producing more hit singles per year than any other label. *Get Ready* was among the Temptations' greatest hits.

made his name as a folk singer writing songs of protest against war and racial injustice. But in 1965 he started to perform with an electric backing group instead of a simple acoustic guitar. His song-writing style changed too and he began to explore a moody, private world of dreams and visions. Dylan brought a new sense of poetry to pop, and his example encouraged the Beatles to write more experimentally.

Above Bob Dylan was an enormously influential songwriter. *Blowin' in the Wind* was among his early protest songs; *The Times They Are a Changin'* became a kind of anthem of the youth revolution.

Above Cult hero Jimi Hendrix helped to change the course of rock music through his astonishing guitar style. But he was also a casualty of the psychedelic era, dying in 1970 from drug abuse.

Psychedelia

Bit by bit the most adventurous pop stars started to lose interest in the kind of music which was aimed at the singles charts. They concentrated more on albums, where they could try out new ideas. The Beatles' *Rubber Soul* (1965) was one landmark, using the music of an Indian sitar on one track. Two years later the group brought out *Sergeant Pepper's Lonely Hearts Club Band*. This was an amazing creation, not only because it had a continuous theme running through it, but also in its use of a brass band, a symphony orchestra and weird sound effects. 'Psychedelia' had arrived.

Psychedelic music aimed to explore different ways of perceiving reality and to suggest dreamy and mystical states. The Beatles did not invent the idea. In San Francisco, groups such as Jefferson Airplane and the Grateful Dead were already closely associated with the hippy movement and were making a new music. The Beach Boys produced a revolutionary album of their own in *Pet Sounds*. In Britain, one of the best-known psychedelic groups was Pink Floyd, who from 1966 used a spectacular light show when they performed live.

Black guitarist Jimi Hendrix also had a huge impact through his psychedelic playing style. He grew his hair out in a wild 'Afro' style too, cultivating a tribal look never seen before on a black performer. New freedoms in music also brought female artists to the fore, including Joni Mitchell and Janis Joplin.

Performers sometimes came together to give free open-air concerts. Out of these grew the first giant rock festivals. Half a million people turned up at the famous Woodstock festival held in August 1968 in New York State, USA.

Above Crowds at Woodstock, 1969. Festivals were a focus of the alternative society. The Woodstock event was held on a farm where half a million people gathered for three days of 'peace, music and love'.

Above Pink Floyd were among the pioneers of psychedelic music. Long instrumental solos and weird electronic effects were part of the style.

Back to bubblegum

By now pop singers were being treated in the media as the leaders of the younger generation. Fans themselves sometimes awaited a new album as if expecting new revelations about the meaning of life. But the stars themselves were finding it hard to live up to the expectations they aroused. The Beatles started to break up as a group in 1969, and in the same year Bob Dylan came out with a very straightforward album of country-and-western songs, called *Nashville Skyline.*

Besides, the whole psychedelic experience had taken pop music a long way from most ordinary teenagers' concerns. After all, young people still needed simple love songs and dance music. There was still 'normal' pop music to be found in the charts. For example, Louis Armstrong had a big hit in 1968 with *What a Wonderful World*. But it was the psychedelic groups who attracted most attention. In reaction against the long-haired groups, record companies started to bring out catchy singles again, aimed especially at younger teenagers. The Archies' *Sugar Sugar,* a smash hit in October 1969, was a classic example of what came to be known as 'bubblegum pop'.

The Media

Above The Monkees were stars of a popular TV series. They were closely modelled on the Beatles.

Teenage music entered everyday life through the cheap transistor radios which had first gone on sale during the 1950s. They were portable, which meant that radio was no longer something that the whole family listened to, grouped together around a large set in the living room. Teenagers could now listen alone in their bedrooms, on the beach or in the street. In the United States, thousands of new local radio stations sprang up. Many played nothing but popular music, and some were more specialized still. There were stations which played only black music, for example, and others playing nothing but country-and-western.

Pirate radio

In Britain the position was different. In the early sixties, broadcasting was controlled by the BBC (British Broadcasting Corporation) which played very little pop music. To hear their favourite records, many teenagers tuned into a European radio station, Radio Luxembourg. This did play solid pop music, but only in the evenings, and reception was fuzzy. But perhaps these difficulties contributed to the special excitement of pop music. In the early sixties it was like a secret known only to the young.

Things changed in 1964 when an illegal, or 'pirate', radio station was set up. Called Radio Caroline, it started broadcasting from a ship anchored off the British coast. Other pirate stations followed, all transmitting non-stop pop to millions of listeners. The pirates were banned by law in 1967 but pop music was now so much a part of British life that the BBC had to set up a new channel to cater for the audience. It was called Radio One, and many of the pirate disc jockeys joined it.

Below A transistor radio on display at a big media exhibition of 1962. In the same year Telstar 1, the first television communications satellite, was launched and transmitted pictures across the Atlantic Ocean.

The Media

Teenage viewers

During the sixties the first live TV pictures were sent across the Atlantic by satellite. It seemed that the electronics media were creating what a Canadian writer, Marshall McLuhan, termed a 'global village'. Millions of teenagers, wherever they lived, might be listening to the same records, wearing the same fashions, doing the same dances. They might be watching the same TV programmes, too, and television played a special part in spreading teenage culture.

For example, the Twist first caught on as a dance craze in the United States after it was seen on the mid-afternoon show *American Bandstand*. When the Beatles first arrived in the United States in February 1964 they were given enormous TV coverage. The cameras followed them as they flew into Kennedy Airport, New York, to be met by thousands of screaming fans. Disc jockeys played Beatles music non-stop and gave updates on their progress through the city. And the climax of the event was their appearance the next night on TV's *Ed Sullivan Show*. It took them into just about every American home.

Favourite TV viewing for American teenagers at that time included *Doctor Kildare,* a series about hospital life. Another cult programme was *Star Trek,* the science fiction series featuring Leonard Nimoy as the pointy-eared Spock. It ran from 1966 to 1969 and reflected the excitement people felt about space exploration.

Britain had its own cult science fiction programme, *Doctor Who,* which first appeared in 1963. And two new pop shows won huge audiences among young people, *Ready Steady Go* and *Top of the Pops.* Both included teenagers dancing in the studio, and so helped to spread fashion ideas.

Below The Beatles on the *Ed Sullivan Show,* 1964. Throughout the United States teenage males switched from short hair to Beatle-style mop-tops.

Above Pop group Manfred Mann perform live on British TV's *Ready Steady Go!* In the early days of this popular programme thousands of teenage mods stormed Television House, hoping to get into the studio.

STARRING
BOB
CUMMINGS
DOROTHY
MALONE
FRANKIE
AVALON
ANNETTE
FUNICELLO
HARVEY
LEMBECK
JODY
McCREA
JOHN
ASHLEY
ALSO STARRING
MOREY
AMSTERDAM
AND
EVA SIX
And Featuring
DICK DALE
AND THE DEL TONES
It's what happens
when 10,000 kids meet
on 5,000 Beach Blankets!
in AMERICAN INTERNATIONAL'S
BEACH
PARTY
IN PATHECOLOR AND PANAVISION®

At the movies

As TV-viewing increased throughout the sixties, movie audiences dropped dramatically. But films still had an influence on teenage culture and reflected the changes that were taking place. In the United States, where many young people had access to a car, a host of cheap films were made to cater for the teenage audiences in drive-in cinemas. The 'Beach' series was particularly successful. The films starred singers Frankie Avalon and Annette Funicello, and included *Beach Party* (1963), *Muscle Beach Party* (1965) and *Beach Blanket Bingo* (1965).

In Britain the American director Dick Lester made two very zany, fast-moving comedies. *A Hard Day's Night* (1964) starred the Beatles, and *The Knack* (1965) was set in the Swinging London of the Carnaby Street era. The style proved so popular that it was copied to make an American TV series *The Monkees.* This in turn proved a great success and the Monkees went on to become international stars who appealed especially to younger teenagers.

During the sixties much more sex and violence was shown on screen than ever before. Older teenagers might go to see one of the James Bond films, which began with *Dr No* (1962). Their mixture of action, humour and expensive sets proved a winning combination with audiences. And the secret agent was a fitting hero at a time when many real-life spy cases were in the news.

Dr Zhivago (1965) was a romantic epic set at the time of the Russian Revolution, and it started a fashion for Russian hats, capes and boots. *Bonnie and Clyde* (1967), about two US outlaws of the 1930s, made gangster clothing fashionable: Bonnie-style berets were particularly popular with young women.

Facing page A poster for *Beach Party.* The film was a big box office hit in 1963 and began a series of further 'Beach' films.

Below *Bonnie and Clyde* set a fashion for gangster clothes, and it also depicted bloodshed and violence more frankly than many earlier films.

Magazines

With so many colourful images flashing at people from screens, the printed word lost some of its impact and importance. The heroes of Batman and Marvel Comics were cult favourites among teenagers world-wide and Snoopy comic books were hugely popular too. Towards the end of the sixties 'alternative magazines' were produced for older teenagers, and often used psychedelic visual effects, such as coloured type and dazzling backgrounds.

There was a great vogue for satire, too. This form of humour ridiculed the stuffiness and prejudices of the older generation. In the United States, *Mad* magazine attracted a big readership. In Britain, the satirical magazine *Private Eye* was founded and poked fun at every kind of Establishment figure, whether in government, the Church, the army or even the Royal Family.

New Freedoms

In the early sixties young people might meet in dance halls, folk clubs or coffee bars. A craze for tenpin bowling spread from the United States, and bowling alleys also became places where teenagers gathered. Surfing was hugely popular on Californian and Australian beaches, though it was hard to find ideal conditions for the sport elsewhere.

Above Surfing in California. The craze had its own slang: a 'hot dog' was a daredevil and a 'wipe-out' was a fall.

Discos and love-ins

The first computer-dating agency made its appearance in the United States in 1965. The idea was to help lonely, single people find partners by recording their details on computer files and bringing together those with interests in common. However, it was many years before this caught on. One new craze that did sweep the world's cities, though, was for disco dancing. The idea came from France where clubs started to emerge in which the dance music was supplied entirely by records played by disc jockeys, instead of live groups. Miniskirted 'go-go' dancers often performed on platforms to set the mood. When psychedelia arrived, dance halls and discotheques started to use flickering strobe lights and other weird lighting effects to create atmosphere.

But why go to dance halls or clubs? Why shouldn't young people simply get together in a park or city square? The idea of holding 'love-ins' spread from San Francisco in the summer of 1967. Long-haired youngsters would gather in groups with no formal arrangements, and would strum guitars, blow soap bubbles or hand out flowers to passers-by as symbols of peace. Often couples embraced and caressed one another very openly. Sometimes, the drug marijuana might be smoked, even though it was illegal.

Events of this type would have been unthinkable in the fifties. Attitudes to behaviour were changing fast.

Below Dancing at a discotheque in 1965. Notice the op art light show. Sometimes, dancers from the floor would get up on platforms to take the place of the professional go-go dancers.

The permissive society

People often speak about a new 'permissiveness' in the sixties. In earlier generations, young people had been given fairly strict guidelines about how to behave in public, what was decent language, which books were fit to read and so on. But now those rules were relaxed. It seemed that almost anything was permitted.

In Britain a new age began in 1960 when Penguin Books decided to publish D. H. Lawrence's novel *Lady Chatterley's Lover* as a paperback. It dealt very frankly with sex, and an attempt was made to ban it. But in court, the jury decided that the book was not obscene. The teacher of a girl's school even testified that it was fit to be read to her pupils. The book went on sale, and after that sex was

Above The cast of the musical *Hair,* photographed in 1968. The story concerned a youth drafted to fight in Vietnam who falls in with some hippies in New York's Central Park. Besides showing nudity onstage it dealt openly with drug-taking.

discussed much more openly in books, newspapers and elsewhere. Censorship of every sort was challenged. Nudity was even allowed on the stage when theatre censorship was abolished in 1968. One of the most famous stage shows at the time was *Hair*. In this, 'the American tribal love-rock musical', some of the actors appeared naked.

During the sixties the contraceptive pill for women also became available. It meant that teenage girls could choose to have sex before marriage, without fear of giving birth to unwanted babies. Abortion was legalized and divorce became much easier. Everything seemed to encourage a carefree attitude to sex and marriage.

New freedoms for women brought new challenges too. The modern feminist movement dates back to about 1966 when the National Organization of Women (NOW) was founded in the United States to win full equality for women in society. A movement campaigning for homosexual rights emerged too.

Schools in the sixties helped to break down outmoded distinctions between races and classes. In the United States, civil rights campaigners pressed hard to get equal opportunities for blacks in education. In Britain there was widespread introduction of comprehensive education in 1965. The system (known as 'one-track' schooling in the United States) was designed to get children

of all abilities mixing together. An upper-class accent was scorned rather than respected by the makers of Britain's youth culture. Many leading celebrities, whether pop stars, photographers, fashion models or film celebrities, had working-class origins.

Traditional religion faced new challenges. Instead of going to church and accepting the authority of the priest or vicar, many young people wanted direct religious experience for themselves. Some took up Eastern religions and the techniques of yoga and meditation. And some experimented with drugs — particularly LSD — to obtain mystical experiences.

Below John Lennon of the Beatles, photographed in August 1967 with the Maharishi Mahesh Yogi. The Maharishi, a Hindu spiritual leader, founded a school of Transcendental Meditation which won many young disciples in the West. The Beatles were followers for a while.

New Freedoms

On the move

Young people often took to the streets in demonstrations, whether against nuclear weapons, racial injustice or the Vietnam War. And demonstrations were not only ways of making political protests. They also brought young people together, and many friendships grew out of such events. People made their opinions felt through badges or 'buttons' with printed slogans, such as 'Make Love, Not War' or 'Black Power'. The button fad began in 1967 in the United States and has never really died out.

Another new freedom lay in travel. Prosperity and advances in tourism meant that young people were able to move around

Below Anti-war marchers, Washington DC. Mass protests brought together huge numbers of people. In America's biggest anti-war demonstration, held on 15 November 1969, some 250,000 marchers converged on the capital.

the world more easily and more cheaply than before. Many young Americans came by jet to visit Europe. In Britain, too, many teenagers were able to take holidays abroad. *Summer Holiday,* a Cliff Richard film of 1962, describes how a group of young London mechanics borrow a double-decker bus to visit the Continent.

Hitchhiking became increasingly popular too. With new interstate highways in the United States, and motorways in Britain and western Europe, it became possible for teenagers to travel long distances overland for free. There was even a dance fad called The Hitchhiker. By the end of the decade long-haired youngsters with backpacks were travelling as far as Afghanistan and India.

Above Hitchhikers photographed in California. Increased travel among older teenagers and students helped to create the idea of an international youth culture. Youngsters with backpacks became a familiar roadside sight.

The cost of permissiveness

The new freedoms created new problems, however, especially through drugs. For one thing, most drugs were illegal and brought users into conflict with police. Furthermore, many people who used the hallucinogenic drug LSD had 'bad trips' — nightmarish experiences — or suffered accidents while hallucinating. Drug overdoses caused quite a number of deaths. Jimi Hendrix, Janis Joplin, and Brian Jones of the Rolling Stones were just a few of the pop stars who died, directly or indirectly, through drug abuse. And in 1969 the press reported a horrific series of murders committed by the members of a Californian hippy 'family' led by Charles Manson. Clearly, drugs and free sex offered no instant solutions to the world's problems. A backlash against permissiveness set in.

Below A rally in London's Hyde Park, 1968, urging the government to legalize 'pot' (marijuana). It is a relatively mild drug, but people argued that society already has enough problems with alcohol abuse.

Youth Cultures

Teenagers in the sixties did not all dress alike and think the same. Different trends led young people in different directions. Separate 'youth cultures' arose, each with their own style of dress, favourite music and type of behaviour. They were almost like different tribes, and some were hostile to others.

Above Long hair and face paints were hippy trade-marks, but by no means everyone adopted the style.

Mods

The first mods emerged in Britain during the late fifties, and became prominent in the sixties. They were usually working teen-agers, often with jobs in offices, shops or banks, who spent their money on stylish clothes. They liked the cool 'modernist' look of imported Italian and French suits. Suede shoes were popular, too. Mods had shortish but carefully cut hairstyles which were sometimes blow-waved or back-combed. The whole look was extremely neat, and true mods bought new clothes incessantly in order to keep ahead of trends. Their ideal was to look perfect all the time.

The boys set the style. Mod girls generally wore rather plain clothes, and a pale-faced look was essential. White lipstick and heavy eyshadow were typical.

The mods made Carnaby Street famous, buying their clothes at a few stylish shops there in 1962-63. They got about on Italian motor scooters — Vespas and Lambrettas — which they decorated with masses of extra lights, chrome mirrors and fur trim. To protect their clothes they wore khaki parkas, which were warm and functional rather than smart. Rhythm 'n' blues (R & B) was the mods' favourite music in the early days. Black American performers such as Muddy Waters and Howlin' Wolf were cult figures. Later, white teenage mods formed groups of their own. The Who and the Small Faces were two well-known examples.

Mods sometimes took amphetamine pills which were then easy to obtain from doctors. Known as 'speed' the drug tended to create a restless energy that often erupted in fights.

Below Scooter-riding mods arrive at the English seaside town of Clacton in Essex, where teenage gangs ran riot in 1964. The big, clumsy parkas were worn to protect the neater clothes underneath.

Youth Cultures

Below A Hell's Angel. Gang members sometimes turned up to act as 'police' at pop festivals, but things occasionally went badly wrong. In 1969 at a free Rolling Stones concert at Altamont near San Francisco a man was stabbed to death by Hell's Angels.

Pent-up aggression was part of the mod experience. Pete Townsend of the Who used to smash his guitar on stage.

In the summer of 1964, masses of mods converged on the English seaside town of Clacton and battles broke out with smaller groups of leather-jacketed 'rockers'. Similar events occurred again in the years to come but by now the true era of the original mods was almost over. Before long, people were using the term 'mod', especially in the United States, to describe anyone young and fashionable.

Rockers and Hell's Angels

Rockers were Britain's leather-clad motorbike riders. Their style of greased hair, leather jacket and jeans went back to the fifties. In fact, rockers tended to be older than the mods, and there were far fewer of them. Rock'n'roll was their music, and they made a point of not following new trends in music and fashion.

In the United States lawless gangs of motorcyclists known as Hell's Angels existed. Some wore Nazi helmets or war medals for shock effect. As the hippy lifestyle caught on in California, the Hell's Angels tended to grow their hair longer. Few of them were teenagers, but by the end of the sixties their style was being copied by small groups of motorcycle enthusiasts in other countries. The term 'greasers' was sometimes used to describe them.

Hippies

In the fifties, 'Beatniks' had often worn sandals, scruffy clothes and longish hair. The hippies came out of this tradition. Jazz, folk music and Eastern mysticism were all part of the movement, as were relaxed attitudes to sex and drugs.

The first hippy communes emerged in San Francisco. They were groups of young people who lived together, sharing their possessions and trying to build something like a tribal lifestyle. It was to be based on co-operation, and offered an alternative to the competitive world outside. In 1967, beads and bells were worn around the neck and flowers were handed out as tokens of peace and love. In the countryside around San Francisco, hippy groups known as diggers emerged, trying to make a living by farming the land communally.

The idea of an alternative society did spread around the world, especially among older teenagers and students. However, few lived a genuine hippy lifestyle. And the Vietnam War made some want to do more than drop out of society; they wanted to change it through marches, demonstrations and revolutionary politics. 'Yippies' was a word coined to describe the political hippies who emerged in the United States.

Below Hippies in love beads and ethnic fabrics relax in a San Francisco park. It was easier to live in a leisurely 'alternative' lifestyle in mid-summer than it was when winter set in.

Black Panthers

The Black Panthers was a revolutionary organization of blacks in the United States. It grew in reaction against the earlier non-violent approach of the black civil rights movement. Few black teenagers were members, but the movement did have a big influence in encouraging young blacks to feel proud of their African origins. Their look, based on leather jacket and beret or Afro hairstyle, was copied even by those who might not share their revolutionary aims.

The Panthers themselves were just one offshoot of the much wider Black Power movement which contained many different groups. Some argued for a return to Africa; others for special Afro-American states to be set up within black American city ghettoes. All aimed to foster a sense of black pride. 'Black is Beautiful' was one slogan, and Afro hair was particularly symbolic. For years, stylish young blacks had been trying to straighten their hair to resemble whites. Now they felt free to express themselves.

Skinheads

In 1969 the British press started to report the presence of a new teenage cult. 'Skinheads' or 'peanuts' shaved their heads almost to the scalp. They wore boots and braces to create a look that was deliberately hard and masculine, or even military. Sometimes skinhead gangs fought one another at football matches; sometimes they beat up long-haired students and hippies.

Skinheads were mostly working youths. They knew they could not expect to get a job if they wore long hair and looked scruffy. Like the mods before them they preferred a clean-cut look, but they took it to extremes.

Psychedelia meant nothing to skinheads. Their views were often conservative. But they were not originally racist. In fact, their favourite music was ska or bluebeat, the early form of reggae. This was the music of black Jamaican youths, played among Britain's large population of ethnic Caribbeans. During the 1970s, however, the skinhead cult became more associated with racist attitudes.

Left The poster shows two Black Panthers wearing the uniform of beret and leather jacket. Panthers claimed that the US government acted like a fascist (extreme right wing) dictatorship towards its black citizens.

Facing page The skinhead look. The turned-up jeans and Dr Marten boots were key items of clothing. Music did not have the importance to skinheads that it did to other cults. The style revolved more around soccer – and violence.

Designs for Living

The background to teenage life changed dramatically during the sixties. City skylines, for example, were transformed. All around the world, huge office blocks built of glass and steel loomed up above older buildings. The number of cars on the roads increased dramatically, causing traffic congestion in many cities. Many new roads were built to ease this problem.

Housing changed too. In many European cities, areas devastated by wartime bombing were created and slums were demolished. Families were rehoused in quickly constructed tower blocks. After the sixties, doubts arose about the quality of life in the new high-rise dwellings. But at the time they seemed to be exciting developments and far superior to the old houses that they replaced.

Above The interior of a flat in fashionable Chelsea, London. Notice the white walls and coarse, fibre flooring.

The modern look

Designers of the time favoured crisp, clean lines in everything that they did. They loved light and space, and tended to avoid anything that suggested clutter or pointless decoration. The concept of 'open plan' living caught on in homes and offices alike. The idea was to have as few walls or partitions as possible. Instead of fussy wallpaper, white walls and ceilings were preferred. In the same way, new houses were built to include big plate glass windows instead of windows with many small panes.

Inside homes, designers employed modern fabrics to create furniture and fittings. There were coffee tables made of clear perspex and coloured plastic, and chairs with tubular steel frames and synthetic upholstery. Instead of pictures with ornamental frames, people hung giant posters on their walls. A poster was cheap and changeable, like so much else in modern mass society.

Below The bare brickwork, see-through table top and wire-frame chairs show taste typical of the sixties 'modern' look. Everything has been reduced to its simplest form to give a sense of light and space.

Below The New York skyline. Skyscrapers had long been distinctive features of American cities. In the sixties, towering office blocks and high-rise flats also sprang up to transform cities elsewhere in the world.

Artists often showed real enthusiasm for mass-produced products. Pop artists, for example, used images taken from comic strips or, as in Andy Warhol's famous picture of soup cans, multiple images of everyday objects. Op artists such as Bridget Riley experimented with abstract designs which created optical illusions. They were often done in black and white, or in bold, flat colours.

Primary colours seemed to fascinate designers. The Union Jack, with its bright red, white and blue, was taken up as a kind of mod emblem during the Carnaby Street years. Pete Townsend of the Who wore a Union Jack jacket. This was partly a satirical gesture, for Britain was losing her world importance. As a growing number of new Commonwealth countries won independence in the early sixties, the imperial flag became a fashion accessory.

Above New York's Museum of Modern Art. The background picture is by Roy Lichtenstein, a pop artist who often used comic strip techniques.

Below Colourful posters appeared in the sixties. Unlike old-fashioned framed pictures, posters were throwaway objects which could be replaced when they lost appeal.

Alternatives

Not everyone liked the ultra modern look. Some people feared what was called the 'technocracy' — the scientists, industrialists and planners who seemed to be dominating every aspect of modern life. There was a great revival of interest in Art Nouveau, the design movement of the 1890s. This had used swirling imagery based on dream symbols, the natural curves of the human body and plant life. Prints by the English illustrator, Aubrey Beardsley (1872-98) became particularly popular.

With the spread of hippy ideas, paisley patterns and Indian fabrics became fashionable. For a tribal or casual effect, teenagers scattered cushions on their bedroom floor. Ordinary beds were disguised as much as possible; divans with fitted covers were thought more stylish. Some teenagers even dispensed with the bed frame and put the mattress on the floor.

Above A teenager's bedroom in the sixties. Notice the Indian bedspread. In the converted fireplace you can see a transistor radio and mono record player.

Young people took to scavenging antique and junk shops for anything cheap with a hint of the quirky or exotic about it. For many older teenage girls, the ideal bedroom look was that of London's Biba boutique, with its old-fashioned bentwood chairs, potted palms and vases filled with ostrich feathers.

Younger teenagers did not attempt anything so sophisticated. Bedroom equipment included a transistor radio, fan magazines and posters of favourite pop stars. If there was a record player it was usually a small, portable device with mono sound. Stereo equipment only came into widespread use towards the end of the decade.

In girls' rooms there was often one item that you would not see today: a gonk. Gonks were cuddly toys with big faces and no body, usually with a Beatle haircut. Teenage girls often made them themselves out of fabric and stuffing. There was such a craze for them in the mid-sixties that a film was made to cash in on the fad. It was called *Gonks Go Beat* (1965) and pop singer Lulu was among the stars.

Images of the Sixties

Man on the moon

On 20 July 1969, US astronaut Neil Armstrong became the first man to set foot on the moon. He was closely followed by his colleague, Ed Aldrin. The pair of them touched down in a special landing craft known as the Eagle, while a third astronaut, Michael Collins, remained in the main spacecraft, Apollo 11, orbiting the moon.

Back on earth an estimated 1,000 million TV viewers watched the event which ended a decade of tremendous advances in space exploration. The Soviet Union had put the first man in space. His name was Yuri Gagarin and he made an orbit of the earth in 1961.

Above The first men on the moon: Ed Aldrin and, reflected in his helmet, Neil Armstrong.

Martin Luther King

Civil rights workers struggled throughout the early sixties to win equality for blacks in the southern states of the USA. Many states operated a policy of 'segregation'. This involved keeping black and white races apart — in schools, housing and buses, for example. Black people were also denied their voting rights. The leading campaigner for civil rights was a black Baptist minister, Dr Martin Luther King. Despite being often beaten and imprisoned, King always pursued a policy of non-violence. His campaigns had real effect and in 1964 he was awarded the Nobel Peace Prize. King was murdered in 1968, however, and his death caused widespread rioting among blacks in US cities.

Above In 1963, Martin Luther King addressed 200,000 people at a civil rights demonstration in Washington DC.

Below The divided city of Berlin. On the left, surrounded by the Berlin Wall and barbed wire, are the sectors controlled by the French, British and Americans. The Soviet sector is on the right.

The Berlin Wall

Throughout the sixties the United States and the Soviet Union dominated world politics. A 'Cold War' was fought between them, with no battles but many angry exchanges of words. Since both sides possessed nuclear weapons, tension was often acute. People feared the outbreak of a war which could end life on the planet.

The divided city of Berlin, deep inside East Germany, was one crisis point. The Soviet authorities controlled East Berlin and in August 1961 built a concrete wall along the boundary with the western half of the city. Some East German refugees were shot trying to cross the Wall, and Soviet and US tanks nearly clashed at a border post known as 'Checkpoint Charlie'. In October 1962, a separate crisis over the siting of Soviet missiles in Cuba almost triggered nuclear war. By the mid-sixties, however, the worst Cold War tensions had eased.

Images of the Sixties

Paris, 1968

In 1968, student riots broke out in the USA, West Germany, Japan, Italy, Britain and France. In Paris, the 'student revolution' nearly brought down the government. The wave of unrest was started by overcrowding and other problems in the education system. But student revolutionaries went on to challenge the whole of French society. In May they took over the Paris university of the Sorbonne, and gave their own classes in the lecture halls. When police tried to storm the building, the students set up barricades in the streets around. Pitched battles were fought, and there were strikes and workers' demonstrations. Weeks later, however, order had been restored.

Above Students and police confront each other outside the university of the Sorbonne in Paris, 1968. Police reinforcements are waiting in the background.

The Six Day War

The Middle East was a troubled region. Since the state of Israel was set up in 1948, two wars had been fought between the young country and its Arab neighbours. In 1967, believing that another war was coming, the Israelis launched a devastating attack on Egypt. The Arab states of Jordan and Syria were drawn into the fighting too.

The conflict lasted for six days in June, and Israel won dramatic victories. Vast new areas were occupied by its troops. But the war left lasting bitterness. In particular, some Palestinian refugees from the occupied territories turned to terrorist tactics to further their cause.

Below A Syrian tank and armoured car stand abandoned near Metulla in Israel, close to the border with Lebanon, following the Six Day War. Israel's third and most decisive victory over the Arabs failed to bring peace.

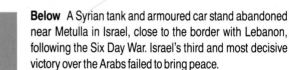

China's Cultural Revolution

China underwent a great upheaval during the sixties. Under the leadership of Mao Tse-tung the country broke with its Communist neighbour, the Soviet Union. Mao believed that the Russians had lost their revolutionary ideals and he wanted to make China a true Communist state, owned and run by its workers and peasants. He used youngsters known as Red Guards as his shock troops. They attacked government officials, university professors and many other privileged people. Some officials were put to work as humble labourers in fields and factories. By 1968, however, disruption was so great that the army stepped in to restore order. Mao's Cultural Revolution came to an end.

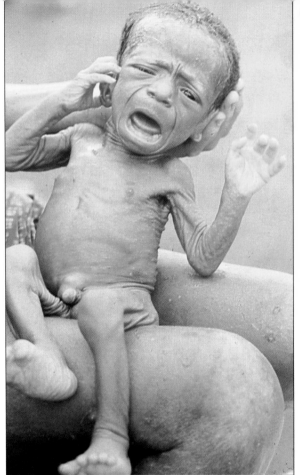

Above An innocent victim of the Biafran War. In addition to those killed in the fighting, thousands of civilians died of starvation and disease.

War in Biafra

A host of European colonies in Africa were granted independence during the 1960s. Among them was Nigeria, which gained independence from Britain in 1960. In 1966, however, massacres of the Ibo people took place in the country, and Nigeria's Eastern Region (which was chiefly Ibo) broke away from the rest of the nation. Under the leadership of Colonel Ojukwu the Eastern Region declared its own independence as the State of Biafra. War, famine and disease followed. Many foreign nations lent aid to one side or the other; some sold weapons to both sides. The fighting ended in January 1970 when the Biafran government collapsed, and Nigeria was reunited.

Above Workers, peasants, children and members of the armed forces salute Mao Tse-tung in this poster from the time of China's Cultural Revolution.

Death of a president

American president John F. Kennedy was assassinated on 22 November 1963 while being driven through Dallas, Texas, in an open car. The event was particularly shocking because the glamorous young president was a symbol of hope for America's future. His New Frontier programme of reform had promised civil rights for black Americans and more help for the needy.

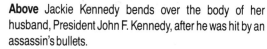
Above Jackie Kennedy bends over the body of her husband, President John F. Kennedy, after he was hit by an assassin's bullets.

Kennedy also concluded a Nuclear Test Ban Treaty (1963) with the Soviet Union, banning nuclear explosions above ground. Some of his acts have been criticized. For example, he contributed to America's drift into the Vietnam War. Nevertheless, his assassination shook the whole world.

The Vietnam War

Since 1954 the country of Vietnam had been divided between the Communist North and non-Communist South. Guerillas from the North had been waging war on the South from the late 1950s. To halt the spread of Communism in the area, the United States started to send in troops, and the numbers grew year by year. About 550,000 Americans were involved by 1969, and thousands of Australians fought too. Massive bombing raids were launched against North Vietnamese cities, but despite the huge effort the Americans could not defeat the guerillas. Peace talks which began in 1968 eventually led to US withdrawal in 1973. The terrible sufferings of the war caused many Americans to doubt their own government's policies and fostered revolt among young people world-wide.

Above A group of wounded American troops on Hill 875, Dak-To. The average age of American soldiers fighting in the Vietnam War was just 19 years.

The first heart transplant

In 1967 a South African surgeon performed the first successful heart transplant operation. Dr Christiaan Barnard took a heart from a 25-year-old traffic victim and placed it in the body of Louis Washkansky, a man suffering from heart disease. The operation, which took 6 hours, astonished the world. However, it was not wholly successful, for Washkansky died of pneumonia some weeks later. Though more heart transplants followed, it proved difficult to keep patients alive for any length of time.

Above In August 1968 the Soviet Union invaded Czechoslovakia. Many people took to the streets in protest, including this boy waving the Czech national flag from the top of a Russian tank in Prague.

The Russian invasion of Czechoslovakia

For many years the Soviet Union had exercised stern control over the countries of Eastern Europe. But in Czechoslovakia a movement for reform emerged when Alexander Dubcek came to power in January 1968. Dubcek wanted more freedom in the press, in business and in the right for Czechs to travel abroad. His reforms worried the Soviet authorities, and in August 1968 Soviet tanks invaded the country. Although ordinary people demonstrated in the streets against the invaders, Dubcek's government was overthrown.

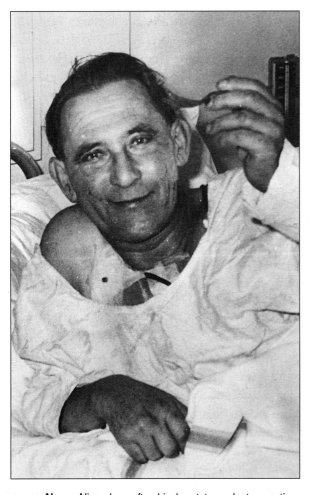

Above Nine days after his heart transplant operation, Louis Washkansky smiles for the camera. Sadly, he died several weeks later.

Glossary

Abortion   An operation to remove a foetus from a mother's womb, so preventing childbirth.

Alternative society   A different kind of society proposed by hippies and others in the sixties. It was to be founded on the principles of love, freedom and complete equality of the races and sexes. It was also known as the counterculture.

Black Power   A movement begun among black Americans to build up black confidence and pursue black interests through united action, rather than seeking help from whites.

Boom baby   Anyone born during the baby boom of the late forties, who became a teenager in the sixties.

Boutique   French word for shop. The term was used in the sixties to describe the new clothing shops catering for youth fashions.

Civil rights   Rights which belong to everyone in a free society, such as the right to vote and the right to a fair trial. The civil rights movement in the United States aimed to win these rights for black citizens.

Cold war   A state of fierce rivalry between nations, stopping short of full-scale war, especially between the USA and the Soviet bloc after the Second World War.

Commune   A small group of people living together and sharing their goods and possessions.

Communism   A political theory aiming to establish a society where the major enterprises such as factories, mines, farms and shops are owned by all citizens rather than a class of wealthy people. In practice, Communist societies have tended to create powerful state authorities which control those enterprises.

Conservative   A word to describe people who wish to hold on to established customs and values, and are cautious about any change.

Contraceptive   A device used to prevent an unwanted pregnancy. The contraceptive sheath, or condom, had long been available for men, but the contraceptive pill for women only became available in the sixties.

Drop out   To refuse to take part in ordinary society, for example by refusing to get a job or to complete a university course, or by avoiding military service.

The Establishment   A grouping of important people and institutions which hold the power in society. Figures include big businessmen, professional politicians, church authorities and army leaders. Overall, their views tend to be conservative.

Feminism   The movement aiming to win full rights and respect for women in society, and to celebrate the special qualities of the female sex.

Freak out   To become highly excited, for example, while dancing at a rock concert. Hippies believed that people should behave without inhibitions, even hysterically if they felt like it, and they did not mind being called 'freaks'.

Global village   A term used by Canadian writer Marshall McLuhan to describe the modern world, reduced to a single community by international communications systems.

Hippy   A member of a Californian commune. It was later used to describe anyone who dropped out, wore long hair or casual clothes, and favoured the ideas of the alternative society.

Homosexual   Someone sexually attracted to members of the same sex; particularly a man who is attracted to other men. Women attracted to women are more often called lesbians.

LSD Lysergic acid diethylamide, a drug which is used in order to experience hallucinations.

Marijuana A drug derived from the hemp plant. It was taken to experience a feeling of well-being known as a 'high', which rarely included hallucinations.

Mod Short for 'modernist', a term for the fashion-conscious working teenagers who emerged in Britain in the early 1960s.

Op art Short for 'optical' art, a form of abstract art based on techniques designed to deceive the eye.

Permissiveness A view of life which holds that people should be allowed to do as they please, with as little interference as possible.

Pirate radio A radio station making broadcasts without authorization from the government.

Pop art A form of art glorifying modern mass-produced images, such as comic-strip cartoons and soup-tin labels.

Psychedelia The distortion of everyday perception of reality through hallucinations and mystical states.

Satire A form of humour ridiculing prominent people, ideas and institutions, especially the Establishment.

Segregation The separation of people according to race, as practised in the southern United States during the early sixties.

Technocracy A system in which society is controlled by scientists and technical experts.

Unisex clothing Clothes designed to be worn by people of either sex, whether male of female.

Further Reading

The 1960s, Tim Healey (Franklin Watts, 1989)

The 1960s, Trevor Fisher, Portrait of a Decade series (Batsford, 1988)

The Sixties, Nathaniel Harris (Macdonald, 1975)

Growing Up in the Swinging Sixties, Susan Cleeve (Wayland, 1980)

Growing Up in the Sixties, Richard Tames (Batsford, 1983)

Life in Britain in the 1960s, Nigel Richardson (Batsford, 1986)

General background

A Short History of the Post-War World, 1945-1970, Duncan Taylor (Dobson, 1977)

The Age of Upheaval; the World Since 1914, J.M. Roberts (Penguin, 1981)

Picture Acknowledgements

Barnaby's Picture Library 5b, 11, 24, 25, 33, 37b; Camera Press 6; Chapel Studios 38t; Kobal Collection 22, 23; Photri 5t, 9, 13t, 20; Popperfoto 4, 13b, 18, 26, 27, 31, 39, 40, 43t, 44t, 44b, 45b; Redferns 12, 14, 16t; Rex Features 7, 15, 16b, 32, 34, 42b; TOPHAM front cover, 8, 10, 17, 19, 21, 28t, 28b, 29, 30, 35, 36, 37t, 38b, 41t, 41b, 42t, 43b, 45t.

Index